AMBIGUOUS DESIRES!

AMBIGUOUS DESIRES!

Loverboy

authorHOUSE®

AuthorHouse™ LLC
1663 Liberty Drive
Bloomington, IN 47403
www.authorhouse.com
Phone: 1-800-839-8640

Published by AuthorHouse   08/27/2013

ISBN: 978-1-4918-0614-2 (sc)
ISBN: 978-1-4918-0734-7 (e)

Library of Congress Control Number: 2013914057

Special thanks to

Grace D. Lundy

for believing in me . . .

CONTENTS

INTRODUCTION

FOR THE LOVER IN YOU . . . ♥ . . . you Know . . . on this night, 04/18/2013, the wind was blowing fiercely . . . as I sit in my convertible BMW, and contemplated the reasons that we are here . . . I was taken by a feeling of loneliness, but my reality was just a few short steps away. It seemed to me that . . . we were all put here to live our lives, and live our lives to the fullest until we *Die*. Was I just put here to die? If so, there is no time to be unhappy . . . in Love . . . out of Love, with whomever we choose. Why would I feel so alone in this vast, wide world? I looked up to the trees and reminisced about the days of old. The country, the way it looked at night when the eyes could only see the moonlight reflect off the tree tops; the feel and the sound of the air, swirling in the branches of the tree tops . . . yea, that nostalgia that only a few of us can still recall. Why make one another unhappy? As I Thanked the Lord for being me . . . As I opened the door on the driver's side, a gust of wind pushed it back in on me. I gave it a shove back! I was almost angered, as I smirked, and thought to myself this wind is ferocious! As I made it around to the trunk of my car, I looked down, and there, lying in the grass, as still as a Rock in the mist of a flowing stream . . . a Card that read . . .

I love you . . .
in so many ways . . .
and for so many reasons . . .
Because you know me . . .
and Understand me . . .
like no one else ever could.
Because you believe in my Dreams . . .
and care about my feelings.
Because you make me Laugh so hard . . .
and smile so often . . .
Because you have a way of bringing out
the very Best in me.

I Love you
in so many ways,
and for so many reasons,
but mostly because
your my very best friend.

Signed By: an AngeL
In closing, I say to you, Prayers carry in the Wind, and Our Father,
hallowed be thy name is Alive, and Well, Beneficent, Merciful and
Proud of his Children! JahMaudi

Onomatopoeia-means the imitation of a sound, in the Greek language the compound word onomatopoeia

TIMBRE'

I MISS you when you're Away . . .
I KISS you when you're not around. I tease you urgently . . .
We dare not make a Sound. ^^()^^ . . . ,
SO You ART to Me . . .
When can I SEE; Why we don't HUG . . .
Just Mean MUGS and Shoulder Shrugs . . .
Those are the Ways of Love*
Random bursts of Energy Flows through my mind.
Your Love Lingers like a Melody . . .
A Genre so Divine . . .
Maybe it's just a Phase; that needs to be Over . . .
Woe . . . Is it True Love that I have Discovered . . .
Either way, there's no stopping now . . .
For the Love we canst acknowledge, I gracefully take a BOW! . . .
I bow out . . .
I bow down . . .
Before fate gets too REAL . . . ,
And validates this Sound . . .
"BOOM!". . .
A Word of Music!

Personal Thoughts

JANUARY

NOW WE KNOW

TO: My Nubian Queen*
What you got ON? . . .
I Want to see you . . .
In your Thong. Unnnn~.
I'm Hung . . .
What's Wrong? Baby . . . Naa,
Yea that's it. Let it go Twurk that . . .
We were meant to be from the Start.
Saturn, Mars, Mercury, Venus, and Jupiter form my HEART.
As Eve was made for Adam, so was my HEART long' for You.
You Art, a Dream Come True.
O'er the Drama, grant ME THE PLEASURE to Measure, your
body's Embrace, your Karma! Heal, your Heart. Let It Go? . . .
It's All right . . .
Cause now "We Know" Dare U Believe . . .
My Heart Beats Tonight! . . .
Ummmm
~>—}—>Loverboy. . . . @U

MERRY X-MAS

Can I Slow Dance with your Mind*
Let's Grind Slow*
Sticky Lust Slow . . .
Ohhh the Trust . . .
Is Between Us . . .
I'm UP! Baby you are so Fine.
You are all that's on My Mind . . .
I Bet! . . .
I can Make You Wet~ . . . .
If you just Let . . .
Me Get into That . . .
Um Cumin Down Ya Chimney Baby . . .
Um Ahh Mercy Mercy Me*
Merry Christmas Baby . . .
~>—}—>Loverboy@U

HOW SILENCE FEELS

You are Completely Loved . . .
Covered in Silence . . .
A Delicate Balance . . .
Your nipples Swell in My . . .
Shhhh Don't Tell . . .
Challenged by a Whisper ~
Ummm . . .
Let Me Love you More . . .
Move Closer ~ As I Adore your Glorious Physique . . .
A Unique Treasure . . .
May I Touch it!!? . . .
Oh* The Silence that Is . . .
>—}—>Loverboy@U . . .

KARMA (REVENGE)

Ohhhh . . .
Sticky Situations Total Stimulations . . .
Text Me Baby . . .
Oh the Drama . . .
When Karma Comes Standing Ovations . . .
Gentle Stimulation . . .
Juices Flowing . . .
Is that Justice Boo . . .
Why Cry with Laughter . . .
Call me After We Do what We got to Do . . .
Playgirl . . .
Oooooh . . .
~>—}—>Loverboy@U

SECRET

Can I Slow Dance with your Mind*
Let's Grind Slow*
Sticky Lust Slow . . .
Ohhh the Trust . . .
Is Between Us . . .
''LUCK'' I'm UP!
Baby you so Fine. You are all that's on My Mind . . .
I Bet! . . .
I can Make You Wet~. . . .
If you just Let . . .
Me Get into That . . .
Um Cumin Down Ya Chimney Baby . . .
Um Ahh Mercy Mercy Me*
Merry Christmas Baby . . .
~>—}—>Loverboy@U

Personal Thoughts

FEBRUARY

RAINY DAYS

Ummm
Where are you on Rainy Days like these . . .
I Need Your LOVE . . .
To Put my Mind @ Ease . . .
Every moment without you is a waste of Time . . .
I cannot get You, Off my Mind . . .
So I Look at your Picture as a Spark* of HOPE!
Just say Yes baby . . .
Never say No. Down on my Knees~
Just the thought of You~ (Muah) Ummm . . .
Sweet and Tender so Much to Do . . .
Surrender your Love!
Ohhh Say It's OK . . .
OK to indulge . . .
To Love this Way . . .
A Kiss a Hug.
O.K to Wish your Wildest Dreams Internal Bliss.
~>—}—>Loverboy@U

HALF MOON ARISING

Half Moon A Rising . . .
Time to Choose . . .
Let Me Know What You Want to DO? . . .
Light/Dark Opposites Attract . . .
IN/OUT . . .
Is that a Fact? . . .
Fast/Slow~Ummm~
Here we Go . . .
Top/Bottom . . . ?
Bed/Floor . . . ?
Front/Back . . . ?
So little Time . . .
The Choice is Yours'.
So make up your MIND*
~>—}—>Loverboy@U

SOUL FOOD

Hey Baby, Lay Back and Relax . . .
Let Me get you in the mood, . . .
Yea, I'm Cooking for You tonight . . .
Some Goode ole Soul Food.
I have a secret recipe, and you know it's Tight! . . .
Along with your favorite Drink, a Bubble Bath, and Candle lights . . .
I'll get the kids to bed . . .
Let me massage your Body . . .
You don't have to move . . . Trust me,
I Got it! You deserve a Break Today
~>—}—>Loverboy@U

MADE FOR YOU

My MIND was made to Understand all the things you
Go Through . . .
My soft Lips* were made to Comfort you . . .
My Arms were made to Hold you . . .
My Hands to Caress and Mold you . . .
My Soul was made to Love you . . .
And You were made for Me . . .
~>—}—>Loverboy@U

LOVE SNACK

Silk PJ's . . .
Chinese Food . . .
and Candle Light on this Rainy Night . . .
Soft Music, Sweet Slow Love, and Peace of Mind ¥ neutrality . . . .
Let's Make it Happen . . . .
Sharing my Soul, To the depths of your reality, How Does It
Feel? Baby~IIIIAHOOOO~
How Does it Feel?
I Wanna Know? . . .
Keeping it Real . . .
~>—}—>Loverboy@U

1, 2, 3, 4.

DON'T COUNT ME OUT BABY,
I COULD BE THE 1.
2. BE THERE FOR YOU.
3. YOU MAY NEED ME
4. EVER HOLD ME CLOSER BABY,
UUUNGH . . .
I'M A SPECIAL KIND.
ENGULFED IN YOUR INHERITANCE YOU SHOULD
BE MINE*
Loverboy>—}—>@U

Personal Thoughts

MARCH

OASIS

O.K., ALL THE WORK IS DONE,
AND IT'S TIME TO PLAY*
WITH YOUR MIND' . . .
IMAGINE THAT! (Intertwined) . . .
YOU AND I ALONE ON A DESERTED BEACH,
WITH NOTHING BUT GRASS AND SAND. LET'S
BUILD A CASTLE ~ . . .
FEEL ME IN YOUR HANDS . . .
AS OUR LIPS MEET IN A SWEET EMBRACE . . .
NEVER TO BE ERASED LIKE THE WAVES OF AN
OCEAN TIDE NEVER STOP WHEN I'M INSIDE
YOUR MIND*
SMMSYESSS***
XXXOOO'S
>—}—>Loverboy @U*

CELIBACY

WAITING FOR ME, TO MAKE A MOVE ~
PULSES RACE~ . . .
AAAUH . . .
YOUR BEAUTIFUL SILHOUETTE . . .
WAITING TO EMBRACE YOUR EBONY SHADES
DELIGHT.
MY INNER SOUL INVITES. ENTICING
DELIGHTS* . . .
BEHOLD A BEAUTY! TO CONSUME MY
FEELINGS OF LOVE.
FOR YOU. SPREAD ON YOU LIKE ROSES ON
ME . . .
NO ONE HAS TO KNOW WHAT WE AGREE TO
KEEP CELIBACY.
~>—}—>Loverboy @*

THE GRIND

WAITING ON YOUR TOUCH, YOUR SMILE,
YOUR STYLE,
YOUR TASTE,
KEEPING UP WITH THIS PACE WON'T BE EASY . . .
SO LET ME SLOW IT DOWN . . .
UMMM . . .
AS THE FEARS SWIRL,
IN OUR SOULS,
LIKE BEING ON TOP OF A FERRIS WHEEL
WAITING TO FALL
IN MY ARMS . . .
R U STILL DOWN?
>—}—> Loverboy @U . . .

REFUND

Psss . . . , It's Me* What's Going on Baby? No ifs, ands,
buts, or maybe's . . . Obviously you are longing for
some . . . Why want? U Come. Missing Me? I'll Kiss U
Blind~ . . . All this School Work is blowing my MIND*, but
Honey, all this MONEY . . . , Uhhng . . . is turning me
ON, making me Horny! . . . *** SMILING ***
Loverboy >—}—> @U

CHANGES

Everything changes somethings just change faster than others . . . ,
Like Lovers . . . ,
All over each other . . .
Brothers/Down for one another . . .
Mothers discover.
Fathers shutter . . .
At the utter of . . .

THUNDER ROAR

IF I COULD APROACH YOU FEEL . . .
AND STEAL YOUR SOUL~
PLEASE YOUR BODY'S WHISPER SOOTH YOUR SOUL . . .
AS SLEEP OVER TAKES YOU, SO CAN I.
DRIFTING INTO YOUR BODY LIKE A THIEF IN
THE NIGHT.
PICTURE THE WAVES, DASHING,
ASHORE . . . OPEN YOUR HEART <3
MY SHEREE AMORE*
LET LOVE FLY FREE, AS THE THUNDER ROAR . . .
I'LL FIND YOU, SLEEP WELL GOODNIGHT ENCORE.
GOODE NIGHT
~>—}—>Loverboy @U . . . .

LET IT DO WHAT IT DO

TONIGHT! IS A NIGHT FOR LOVERS . . .
WRAP YOUR BODY TIGHT UNDER THE COVERS . . .
DISCOVER A WORLD FOR ME AND YOU . . .
WHERE EXSTACY AWAITS . . . LEST WE DO; WHAT
WE DO? . . .
UMMM RIGHT THERE; RIGHT THERE!
THAT'S THE SPOT. DON'T STOP,
DON'T STOP: KEEP IT HOTT
YOU GOT THAT; WHAT I WANT
SO GIVE IT TO ME BABY~
AAAH YEA
~>—}—>LOVERBOY .@U . . .

Personal Thoughts

APRIL

LOVE ESSENTIALS

LOVE is ESSENTIAL TO LIFE . . .
YOU CAN'T DENY LOVE . . .
WHEN YOU DO . . .
IT CAN COME BACK TO HUNT YOU . . .
EVERYTHING WILL MAKE LOVE TO YOU . . . .
LOVERBOY
>—}—> @U

VALENTINE 2011

VALENTINES DAY HAS CHANGED 2011,
BUT 1 THING STAYS THE SAME . . .
"LOVE," . . .
LOVE IS GREATER THAN HATE, JUST AS GOODe
IS GREATER THAN BAD . . .
SO, IF WE ALL AS THIS F.B.
FAMILY CAN HAVE A GROUP HUG,
AND COME TOGETHER ON 1 ACCORD,
FOR THIS YEAR . . .
NEW BEGINNINGS . . . .
IS THE FUTURE . . . .
SALON7SPA@GMAIL.COM

CANDY FANTASIES

WILL U B MY VALENTINE? . . .
GIVE ME YOUR HEART and SOUL.
MINE . . .
FOR JUST A LITTLE TIME . . .
SECRET CANDY FANTASIES*
BETWEEN U and I . . .
TELL ME WHAT U WANT AND I'LL BE YOUR DESIRE . . .
LEAD ME TO YOUR SECRET PLACE AND LET HOT,
EROTIC, STEAMY, PASSIONATE LOVE GUIDE THE WAY . . .
TO YOUR, G-SPOT!!!
WE'RE ALMOST THERE
>—}—>Loverboy @U*

Personal Thoughts

MAY

YES

YOU ARE SO BEAUTIFUL.
INSIDE AND OUT.
DOUGHT PLAYS A SILLY GAME.
I WON'T.
LOVE'S SUCESS EXCLUSEVELY: I'D CLEAVE TO YOU.
CATCH YOUR BREATH
MY DEPTH, PLEASING, TEASING, EASING YOU, UNGH . . .
RIGHT THERE.YEA, YEA, YEA. I SWEAR!
WILL YOU COMFORT ME?
ALL YOU HAVE TO DO IS SAY
~>—}—>Loverboy @*

WITHOUT YOU

I KNOW YOU MISS ME, SSSS (MUAH) . . .
I MISS U TOO. SO MUCH LOVE (Smuah),
WHAT ARE WE GOING TO DO?
DYNASTY SEPERATES US, I CAN'T BE RULED.
TIME HAMMOCKED BACK AND FORTH,
FOR THE NIGHT'S EXTRA HOUR,
FOR ME TO UWWWH,
YOU TILL KINDOM COME,
I'LL BE YOUR JEWEL
THE MORNING SUN
DIAMOND IN THE RUFF,
I AM A GIRLS BEST FRIEND.
OPEN YOUR UNGH,
AND LET ME IN.
TO YOU, UNGH. HOW CAN I,
EXPLAIN, HOW CAN I GO ON . . . ?
~>—}—>LOVERBOY@u*

THE DON

FIRST DAY OF CLASS, I KISSED' YOU.
I'M SO STRESSED, I MISSED YOU . . .
I'm Done' T'EVEN, WANT TO FUSS . . .
I LOVE YOU SO MUCH; SECRETLY HOLDING YOU,
IN MY HEART. YOU'RE THE OBJECT OF PURE DESIRE.
CURSING IN PLEASURE. DAMN! . . .
YOU CUTE . . .
OH SSSSH'T . . . .*
***~>—}—>LOVERBOY@U

WAIT ON ME!

WHEN THE LIGHTNING FLASH! . . .
WAIT ON ME . . .
UMM THUNDER ROLL . . .
SO TRUE TO THEE. FEEL THE WONDER . . .
AS OUR CLOUDS' EMERGE.
FEEL THE POWER AS YOUR HEART SERGE!
~ ENERGIES~ELECTRIFY TO INTENSIFY YOUR URGE.
BOOOM!
YOU'RE TREMBLING UNGH;YOU HEARD,
THE SOUND; FOREVER AND ALWAYS, YOU
WON THE ROUND . . . ,
BUT HERE I COME AGAIN,
LIGHTNING FLASH . . . !?!!
WAIT . . . ON ME
->—}—>LOVERBOY@U . . .

NAKED

EXCUSE ME MISS, ARE YOU ALONE?
TONIGHT YOU'RE MINE . . .
I'M THE ONE.
CAN'T HELP BUT STARE, YOUR EYE'S MESMERIZE ME?
THEY HIDE ME WHEN YOU'RE NOT THERE.
SPELLBOUND*
HEAVEN DRESSED, CARESSED, PRETTYEST . . . .
YOUR HAIR, YOUR YEAA . . .
UOOO YOU SO FINE . . . $,
AND IF YOU WERE MINE . . .
I'DE BE THERE . . .
WOOOO . . .
THE WAY HEAVEN DRESSED.
THE LORDBLESSED . . . ,
SMILE,.
UNTIL THEN . . . ,
I LOVE YOU! . . .
ETERNALLY
LOVERBOY~>—}—>@

Personal Thoughts

JUNE

STEPPER'S GROOVE

HEARTBEAT . . .
DANGER . . . .
DECIDE . . .
I'VY GOT MY PRIDE! . . .
MY BRIDE . . . .
IM ON THE PROWL . . . .
MILE AFTER MILE I'LL HUNT, YOU DOWN?
DON'T GET SACRED NOW . . . ,
I WANT YOU! . . . .
YEA . . .
YOU KNOW WHO . . .
GO IN THE PANNY DRAW . . .
THE PANIC DR.O . . .
WHO SAW?
GIRL YOU SO WILD . . . , , ,
SO SOFT, SO SWEET, I'M ON THE PROWL
~>—}—>LOVERBOY@U

HATER ALERT

HATER ALERT::::
I REPEAT, HATER ALERT::::
BE CAREFUL!
THE SEASON IS CHANGING'
AND THE SNAKES ARE SLITHERING,
BACK TO THERE HOLES . . .
BE CAREFUL HOW U DRESS,
CAUSE ALL THEY CAN DO IS SHED THEIR DEAD SKIN . . . .
REAL TALK . . .
SO IF YOUR FALL WARDROBE IS MEAN,
LIKE MINE,
YOU MIGHT WANT TO INVEST IN A GOOD
KNIFE OR A CAN OF MACE . . . .
THEY SAY MOTH BALLS IS GOOD TOO . . . REAL
TALK FAM . . . .

I DO

LOVERBOY HERE FOR YOU;
THROUGH YOUR OPPOSITIONS.
ADJUSTING TO YOUR NEEDS.
CHANGING, POSITIONS.
LOVING YOU SOFT.
AS GENTLE AS HE CAN.
THE GENTLEMAN IN ME!
DO YOU UNDERSTAND . . . ,
WHAT IS IT THAT YOU WANT?
AND ALWAYS DEMAND . . .
WHAT GOOD IS KNOWLEDGE IF
YOU DON'T UNDERSTAND . . .
I LOVE TO NEED YOU,
WANT TO,
GOT YOU, HAVE YOU . . .
Hmmm*SMILE*.
~>—}—>LOVERBOY@U

LOVE

LOVE IS WHY GOD MADE YOU,
FOR MY EYES TO SEE,
A VISION OF PERFECTION,
SO YOU ART TO ME.
TIME BECKONS WITH YOU,
AND NEVER ENDS.
DANCING CLOSE TO YOU,
AND BEING YOUR FRIEND.
PICTURE PERFECT,
FACE TO FACE.
THE FRAME IS MADE OF IVY LACY,
A WARM EMBRACE.
A PASSIONS' CHASE,
A FLAMING SWORD!
CHERUBIMS DO PROTECT,
THIS LOVES' REWARD.
~>—}—>LOVERBOY @U

THE SYLLABUS

LOVERBOY,
WANTS TO CLEAR THE AIR,
ITS BEEN SAID THAT LOVERBOY IS A PLAYA . . .
NOT TRUE: HE'S A LOVER NOT A FIGHTER . . .
A SLAYA, NOT A PLAYA . . .
A LAYA NOT A PLAYA . . .
A STAYA, NOT A PLAYA,
A PAYA, NOT A PLAYA . . . .
SO LOVERBOY,
LOVES TO SLAY LAY STAY,
AND PAY, AND I JUST MAY , . . .
BUT NOT PLAY . . .
O.K.
WHO'S READY?

Personal Thoughts

JULY

PUSSY CAT

euwww . . . esssss . . .
SO COLD*,
WILL YOU HOLD ME?
COVER ME, WITH YOUR TOUCH.
MY BODY'S CALLING,
I WANT YOU SO MUCH.
UMMH, ITS SLOW SO, SPEAK LOW.
PLEASE DON'T RUSH.
I FOUND YOUR G $POT,
CREAM IF U MUST!
I KNOW THE COMBINATION . . . ,
TO GET YOU WET, click' click' click'
LICK STICK, TURN.
Ahhhhh, CATCH YOUR BREATH,
WE JUST BEGUN . . .
Oooo, YOU'RE SO HOT!
~>—}—>LOVERBOY @U

EROGENOUS MOON

EROGENOUS MOON, FIRMAMENT INDUCED INTRICATE PLEASURES. SPONTANEOUS IMPULSES BEYOND ALL MEASURE; AROUSED BY NATURE. H€AR THE THUNDER ROAR!! FALL SECRET DESIRES, WE DO ADORE;' COME TO ME' SURRENDER YOUR WILL! FILL MY POWER! AS TIME STANDS STILL! FEEL THE PASSION, FEAR THE PAIN. HEAR MY HEARTBEAT, SOUNDS THE SAME. FALL FROM THE SKY, O' FULL MOON, AND LAY DOWN BESIDE ME. BRIDE AND GROOM.

SUBDUDED

FULL IS THE MOON . . .
STILL, IT LOOK LIKE MY SWEET STAR DON'T FEEL
THREAT MY DEAR . . . .
MY SOUL IS HERE, FOR I STAVE THE WEREWOLF,
AND CONQUER THE NIGHT . . . WISH YOU WERE HERE
SMILE

WET APPETITE

MY APPETITE IS WET . . . ,
LIKE YOUR TIGHT WET, UMMM, YEA I BET . . . ! UMMHU.
SQUEEZE, STOP, PULL . . .
DROP! SQUEEZE, HOT, CLINCH, POP!
TELL ME HOW YOU WANT ME TO STOP!
LET IT GO, NO DON'T STOP!
YOUR BODY IS SO BEAUTIFUL, TOUCH IT!
DARE NOT! "STOP,
NO, DON'T, STOP, NO, DON'T STOP!"
FEEL THE URGE, TASTE THE AIR.
TONGUE TO TONGUE. (Gnulp)
WHAT'S THAT LIKE? (gnulp, gnulp)
TASTE YOU THERE;
I JUST MIGHT, WET YOUR APPETITE!
~>—}—>LOVERBOY @U'

IN TIME

UMMM, I WANT YOU, YOU WANT ME:
YOUR DEEPEST, DARKEST, DESIRE: DEEPLY, WET,
PERSPIRE.
MYRR, INCENSE, OIL, THRUSTING HOT PASSIONS BOIL.
LYE ON MY CHEST, AS I CARESS,
THE FINE HAIRS UMMM . . . ,
ON YOUR NECK: BACK, BUTT, LEGS;
AND BREAST.UUNNGH~ BABY, I'M THROBBING . . . ,
THOBBING!
THROBBING SO HARD.
CONTEMPLATE, WAITING, TO BE YOUR STAR
* TURN THE LIGHTS DOWN LOW,
uuuh SO GOOD, SO Goode IT FELT,
AS THE CANDLE WAX MELT!
~>—}—>LOVERBOY

Personal Thoughts

AUGUST

THE AROMA OF LOVE

IT'S CHRISTMAS EVE GIRL,
LETS CURL BY THE FIRE . . .
HOT, COZY, AND WARM.
YOUR LONELY BODY, SPARKS DESIRE. ENGULFING
FLAMES OF PASSION'S BURNING SECRETS SUBLIME.
LET ME LEARN IN TIME.
UMMM SENSUAL PULSES ELUDES OUR TOUCHES,
SUFFICE OUR MINDS INTERTWINE IN TURMOIL
OUR CRISES RISE.
TONGUE KISSES OPT;
WE DARE NOT. TOO HOT TO STOP::
TOP FLESH ON FLESH, SWEAT, WET,
AS WE CHURN . . .
THE AROMA OF LOVE~
>—}—>LOVERBOY@

YOUR WET DESIRE

ENHANCE MY STEEL BOW . . .
WE WANT THE SAME.
WAKE UP, MY DEAR, FREE TO DREAM. PLESURE AWAITS
YOUR TOUCH, SERENE. THUMP . . . THUMP.
ARE YOU THERE?
FEEL MY SURGE, I AM HERE. UMMM'
YOUR URGE! LET IT GO.
I'LL SUCK, IT MIGHT, YOUR NECK,
YOUR THIGHS, THAT'S RIGHT!
TEST IT: TASTY FORWARD NIGH . . . ,
ENOUGH TONIGHT.
YOUR WET DESIRE.
DROP IT LET:
~>—}—>LOVERBOY @U

TIME CONSTRAINTS

WAITING . . .
INSIDE YOUR LOVE.
TIME, CONSTRAINS US . . .
SECRETS!
HIDE YOUR EYES . . .
PATIENCE IS YOUR DISGUISE.
TAKE A DEEP BREATH.
FEEL ME . . . ! NOW?
Butterflies
RIGHT THERE, WAITING INSIDE,
WANTING INSIDE YOU.
UNHG . . .
SO DEEP DESIRE YOUR PRESENSE INSPIRE.
THE CLIMAX!!! . . .
UMMMM . . .
HOW DOES IT FEEL~BABY . . .
~>—}—>LOVERBOY@U

TRUE TO THEE'

WHEN THE LIGHTNING FLASH! WAIT ON ME . . . UMM
THUNDER ROLL . . .
SO TRUE TO THEE. FEEL THE WONDER . . .
AS OUR CLOUDS EMERGE. FEEL THE POWER AS YOUR
HEART SERGE! ~ ENERGIES~ELECTRIFY TO INTENSIFY
YOUR URGE. BOOOM!
YOU'RE TREMBLING UNGH;YOU HEARD,
THE SOUND., FOREVER AND ALWAYS, YOU WON THE
ROUND . . . ,
BUT HERE I COME AGAIN,
LIGHTNING FLASH . . . !?!!
WAIT . . . ON ME~
>—}—>LOVERBOY@U . . .

OH!

MY GODDESS. CURL MY TONGUE IN YOU, . . . EASING,
TEASING, PLEASING YOU, SOFT AS THE WINDS' TOUCH.
WISPERS CONNECT.
(I LOVE YOU SO MUCH).
YOUR HAIR, YOUR BREAST, THE TINGLING, WHAT'S
NEXT.
Shhhh . . . SMAUH, YOUR NECK.YOUR NAKED DIALECT
SEX.
Ahhh. WHAT THE HECK . . .
CAN I BITE YOU SOFTLY, PLEASE SAY YESSS . . . SSSSSS,
THERE YOU GO . . .
UMMM SLOW, DIVULGING YOUR SECRET PALACE.
AND PLACE MY PHALLUS . . .
PLEASE?
~>—}—>LOVERBOY@U

Personal Thoughts

SEPTEMBER

EQUILLIBRIUM

YOU IN THE BED?
WELL GET COMFORTALBE AS YOU MAY.
I WANT TO HOLD YOU, AS WE LAY;
YOU KNOW; WHERE YOU WANT ME!
YOUR SECRET DESIRE . . .
YOUR ENIGMA INTRIGUES ME . . . ,
EXCITING, INVITING, BITING.
WANTING MORE.
YOUR CHOC 'LATE DESIRE,
THAT MISSING PEACE.
TO YOUR PUZZLE. IT FITS,
SO, LET'S NUZZLE, LIKE ESKIMOS DO.
(Gasp) YOU WANT ME,
LIKE I WANT YOU . . . !
~>—}—>LOVERBOY@U

THE CRUSH

SOMETIMES YOU WISH YOU NEVER HAD . . . ,
BUT ALWAYS WANT, WHAT U NEVER HAD, DON'T GET
MAD.,
CAUSE YOU ARE SAD,
AND STOP WHAT COULD HAVE BEEN.
KEEP YOUR DIGNITY AND BE FRIENDS . . . , CAUSE ONE
DAY, ONE HOUR, ONE MINUTE ONE SECOND, OF YOU, IS
GREAT, IN THE END . . . I APPRECIATE . . .
THE LOVER IN YOU . . .
~>—}—>LOVERBOY@ll IN. U?

SO SWEET

PSSSEE . . .
GONE GET IN THE SHOWER.
AS THE WATER BEATS DOWN ON YOU,
I'LL BE THERE . . .
EVERY DROP SATISFIES YOUR MIND, BODY, AND SOUL,
LOOSE CONTROLL, LET ME IMMERSE YOU IN DIVERSE
PLEASURES!!! STIMULATING EVERY INCH OF YOUR BODY,
AS I MEASURE:
YOUR ANATOMY PLEASING ME . . . .
ARE YOUR NIPPLES HARD?
I'M HERE TO SATISFY, YOUR RESPONSE, YES. THINK OF
THE POSSIBILITIES. ~
>—}—>oouuwww. YOU SO WET . . . !
LOVERBOY@U

FORGIVE SLOW

Psss. COME FORTH MY LOVE, REMOVE THAT GOWN.
YOUR SMILE WILL SUFFICE. DON'T MAKE A SOUND.
(shhh), TOUCH YOUR BODY, YOUR SKIN SO SOFT.
WAIT . . .
WAIT . . . .
FEEL THE VIBE~
LET OUR ENERGIES CROSS~. SWEET/HARD/WET, LET,
LOVE LUST. EEE, UMM . . . Ahh. GIVE IT TO ME! TAKE
WHAT YOU MUST!
O O, O O OOW*,
DON'T BE AFRAID!.
>—}—>LOVERBOY @U

ONLY WE KNOW

CAN YOU STOP THE WIND FROM BLOWING,
OR MY LOVE FROM SHOWING;
WHY FATHOM AN IDEA;
BABY I'M HERE, HAVE NO FEAR,
FREE YOURSELF TO BE, GLOW WITH ME.
LET LOVE LEAD YOU, LET ME PLEASE YOU . . .
FAITH IS PLEADING TRANQUILLITY, THAT GUILTY
SMERK~HUMILITY, YEA, THAT ONE,
OF ECSTASY . . .
WHY INTERFERE WITH LOVE?
CAN YOU STOP THE RAIN FROM ABOVE?
NOR CAN YOU STOP MY LOVE.
IT'S CALLING . . . ,
ANSWER . . .
>—}—>LOVERBOY @U

Personal Thoughts

OCTOBER

A PRISONER OF LOVE

BE MINE! . . .
MY LOVE, A GENEROUS GRIND.
BODY'S WET!
CLINCHED TO MINE . . .
DRENCHED IN SWEAT,
A SILHOUETTE OF LOVE.
MY PIECE IN YOUR PEACE,
LIKE FEATHERS ON A DOVE . . . UUNGH.
BABY . . . UUNGH . . . ,
DON'T STOP THIS FLOW,
Umm. TASTE MY HUNGER,
FEEL IT GROW.
UUMMM YOU'RE TREMBLING LADY,
CLOSE YOUR EYES . . .
CAPTIVATED LOVE SWELLS INSIDE . . .
CAN YOU FEEL ME . . .
A PRISONER OF LOVE.
.>—}—>LOVERBOY@U

FOLLOW THE INSTRUCTIONS

MY APPETITE IS WET . . . ,
LIKE YOUR TIGHT WET, UMMM, YEA I BET . . . !
UMMHU . . . SQUEEZE, STOP, PULL, DROP! SQUEEZE,
HOT, CLINCH, POP!
TELL ME HOW YOU WANT ME TO STOP!
YOUR BODY IS SO BEAUTIFUL,
TOUCH IT!
I DARE!
FEEL THE URGE.
TASTE THE AIR.
TONGUE TO TONGUE. (gnulp)
WHAT'S THAT LIKE?
(gnulp, gnulp) TASTE YOU THERE;
I JUST MIGHT.,
TURN OFF THE LIGHTS!
~>—}—>LOVERBOY @U'

HIGHER STANDARD

YOU HOT' YOU READY,
WAIT. EUWHH . . . WAIT . . .
CLEAR YOUR MIND.
WE HAVE TIME, CAUSE TONIGHT BABY,
I'M YOURS.
LET ME RUB YOUR BACK,
SUCK YOUR TOES,
AND DO ALL THE . . .
THINGS, EUUUWW HE DIDN'T KNOW . . .
OOOH . . .
TASTE YOUR OOOOH ON MY TONGUE,
FEEL YOUR OOOH, OH SO WARM . . .
WAIT BABY, I'LL BE THERE
~>—}—> U KNOW OHHH
LOVERBOY CARES @U

INTO YOU

THE MOON IS FULL,
LIKE MY LOVE FOR YOU,
BUTTERFLIES DANCE,
AS WE ROMANCE,
A FORBIDDEN FRUIT,
AS MY STOMACH TOUCHES YOURS, (SKHIN)'STICKING
TO YOU, BUTTERFLYS RACE,
QUICKENS THE PACE . . .
IM SO IN. ARE YOU!
A SECRET LOVE . . . .
~>—}—>LOVERBOY @*

BUTTER LOVE

MESSING UP YOUR HAIR,
PULLING YOU CLOSE TO MINE.
FACE TO FACE, AS WE EMBACE . . .
I KISS YOUR LIPS,
SSSLWEEEERP TONGUE,
SSSLEEEERP TONGUE,
HEADED DOWN SOUTH,
POP, POP, SLREEERP, POP.
UNNNmmm.
DON'T STOP, I NEED YOU . . . .
LOVERBOY~>—}—>@U

Personal Thoughts

DECEMBER

READY OR NOT

HOLD YOUR PILLOW TIGHT . . .
SQUEEEZE, WITH ALL YOUR MIGHT . . .
WRITING THAT . . .
UMMM, I CAN'T LET GO . . . YOU MOVE;
I SCRREEEAAAMMM!!!
SEEMS LIKE A DREAM, UNDER YOUR COVERS,
IN YOUR BED,
SLOW AND STEADY . . .
YOU THOUGHT I WAS THROUGH,
I THOUGHT YOU WERE READY . . . !
LOVERBOY>—}—>@ YA

SERIOUS AS THE SNAP!

MAMA, . . . I'M DEEP WITH THE DRAMA . . .
CALL IT KARMA . . .
SOCRATEASE:
YOU KNOW THE NAME,
WHO'S TO BLAME' DAMN SHAME . . .
WHOOSH THERE IT IS . . .
LULABY BABY, LULA 'BYE . . .
CALM INSTINCT . . .
CARCENOGENARATION LOVE . . .
AGUST A MEN . . . .
DOVE . . . .
YOU CAN HATE ME NOW . . . .
I'M SO REAL . . .
LOVERBOY
~>STING—}—> @ YA.!

INTERMISSION

EVEN THOUGH YOU MAY BE SLEEP,
WAKE THA'SS UP. HUMMMm,
AS WE SHOWER.
HUNNNN, ITS ME.
TAP, TAP, TAPPING, SOFTLY,
WATER RUNNING . . .
WHISPER~ psshhhhh.,
COME HERE, MOVE CLOSER,
JUST WANNA HOLD YOU,
SHHHH WAIT . . . !
IT'LL COME . . .
WHATEVER, IT'LL COME . . .
MMMmmmm . . . .
>—}—>LOVERBOY @U*

التَّيَّمُ (LOVE)

THE MOON IS HALF,
YES I STAND,.
TO QUENCH MY THIRST,
THE MAN IN THE MOON,
DUSK COME FIRST LOVE . . .
Quickly MOVE IN SLOW . . .
QUICKLY SO I MOVE SO SLOW,
SO HOLD ME TIGHT DON'T LET GO.
THROUGH THE NIGHT,
ROUND AND ROUND AND ROUND WE GO,
FASTER FASTER, FASTER,
NOW SLOW,
ROUND AFTER ROUND,
KEEPING UP THIS FLOW . . .
LOVERBOY (UNGH)
LET GO
-̃>—}—>YUISH @U.!

FEEL THE RUSH

YOU AND I, ALL ALONE,
DESERT ISLE, NOW YOUR HOME
TOES SHRED SAND,
FEEL THE RUSH!
HAND AND HAND,
YOUR FATE BLUSH . . .
WOMAN, I'M THE MAN . . .
FEEL THIS PLEASE,
DON'T FUSS, AS THE TIDE RISES,
WE WASH ASHORE . . .
CRASHING WAVES,
CLOTHE OUR SOLES.
CLOSE THINE EYES,
AND BEHOLD,
THE WATER RIPPLES
FEEL THE BRUSH . . .
ACROSS YOU . . .
WE ARE NEAR, PIERCING,
OUR EDEN . . .
CLOSE YOUR EYES . . .
~>—}—>LOVERBOY .@U

CHIVALRY

Sch . . . Sch . . . Sch . . . Chivalry isn't Dead!
As Chills exacerbate my Body!
I Offer you my gladness, the warmth of a Smile;
To take away the edge of the Cold and Sadness.
I gladly give to you the Melody of the Birds . . .
Chirping to comfort your Lonely Heart!
T'wart my character is True
To embrace your innocence . . .
As a Sword in a Stone . . .
Making what tis Right not wrong!
The Chills Grow and comfort me as
I extend my Hand to you . . .
A touch to separate what tis Good from what tis Bad!
Making the unknown known
And what once was Hard, Soft again!
Loverboy>---}-->@

HOT!

Rrrr Rrrr Rr Rrrr (the rooster crow) . . .
Good Morning Babe let me be your Cup of Coffee . . .
Something to get you started off right.
Use as much Sugar as you Like
(Muah) (Muah) (Muah), ssssss
Is that Enough?
Can you Cream for Me.
Gradually staring, slowly stirring . . .
Stir it Up . . . Stir it Up. Stir it up Blow!
Now Sip (seewp) . . . Good Job!
Taste me! As I touch your Lips.
Into your Mouth and Down your throat.
To warm your Mind, Body, and Soul!
Was it Good to You Baby? Oh, it was Good!
Down to the last Drop! (Plop)
>---}-->Loverboy@U

BOBBY

A Jang a Lang, A jang a lang,--
Ah; Excuse Me, Ah, Excuse Me,
Can you spare some change?
The State of the economy is driving me insane . . .
Go Get a Job Buster! Leave me a loan . . .
I Have a Job, Go Get your Own.
A jang a lang, A jang a lang,
Can you spare a Dime?
Sure, and here is some More, to buy- you some Time.
Here you Go, have a pleasant Day . . .
A jang a lang; A Jang a lang,
Now be on Your Way. With a Trillion Dollar Debt,
It Should be Easy to DO!
A jang a lang, a jang a lang,
Which one are You?
Goodbye, A Jang a Lang . . .
>---}-->Loverboy@U

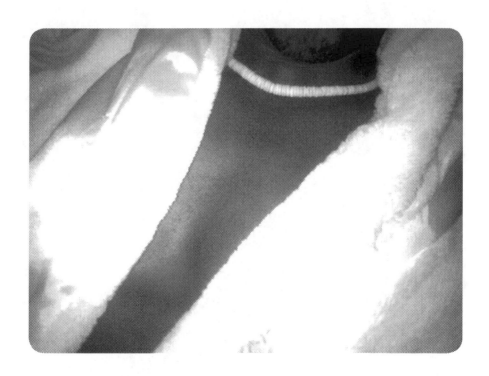

LOVER'S MAZE

```
L C G N I Y P V X C E R P Q D F K J N Z W
E X O T I C E U S S R O B Z X T L T A C C
L S E L O V E R B L E A D O R E D O M U R
O T G A D O P I T I M I S T I C D V E V T U
V R O M A N T I C F R E A K Y E A T Q E S
E A D O T A D B M O V I E S C L M D A Y H
R W D N I F E I F G Q U E E N I B H M I P
B B H Y N J L K C L Y H D H V S I E B M N
O E I T G S M I L E G U O A I E G R T Q O
Y R I E P N U O R P U G O R R N U O N R C
S R C T U C U M A T H S G M T S O G E S T
K I S S E S R V M X A Y Z O U U U E G E U
N E O N A E B E C M P T D N O A S N I S R
N S N E E X Y F A G P H I Y U L K O L O N
D T I T J K L M N M Y O P O S L I U L R A
C A Q A D E L I C I O U S R U S N S E Y L
T L T L U V X C A N D Y Y F Z S K A T O Y
U K J O Y F U L D A S S I B E C Y D N J S
R O H C T E D D Y T I T S C E F E G I U A
A Z I O J E E D I P U C A K P Q N A B A T
I B E H P T C H N A Z E S E X Y O L O E N
C H O C O L B P E I P J L B E T M Y B B A
N D E S I R E B O O K C O A R Y C O Z Y F
```

ADORE	FLIRTATIOUS	NICE
AMBIGUOUS	GOOD	NOCTURNAL
BEAUTIFUL	GOODE	OPTIMISTIC
BOOK	HAPPY	PEACE
CANDY	HARMONY	QUEEN
CHOCOLATE	HUGS	ROMANTIC
COZY	INTELLIGENT	ROSES
CRUSH	JOYFUL	SENSUAL
CUPID	KIND	SEXY
CUTEY	KISSES	SMILE
DATING	LOVE	STRAWBERRIES
DELICIOUS	LOVER	TALK
DESIRE	LOVERBOY	TEDDY
EROGENOUS	MONEY	UMMM
EXOTIC	MOVIES	VIRTUOUS
FANTASIES		WHIPCREAM

YO COFFEE BEAN

Let me be your Coffee Bean Baby , , ,
GRIND me Up Slow . . .
Melt me Down in some Boiling Hot Water Baby, and Watch me
Grow . . .
"Expansion" . . . Did I forget to mention? . . .
GRIND ME! . . . GRIND ME! . . .
I'm Yo Coffee Bean Baby . . .
Taste me in the Moaning . . . I'LL Behave . . .
Taste me in the Evening . . . I'LL Be your Slave . . .
Don't Beat around the Bush . . . Taste Me RAW!
A BITTER/SWEET . . . GIVE Me Some of That! NO! . . . Nah . . .
Taste Me Moving, Crave My Energy . . .
Aww. Baby, Give Me Some of Dat*
Yo Coffee Bean . . .
>---}-->Loverboy@U

DENIAL

(Muah) Baby, Muah Let's gets past this . . .
Dammit! How many times must I apologize for the same thought! I
hurt you over and over again . . .
Butterflies arise . . . You said you liked it . . .
You offered me your honesty . . .
You said harder, and harder. Memories, I trusted you. Now you hold
it against me. Why canst we stop! Why can't we pass over this? Cause
we don't want to Stop! The future
>---}-->Loverboy@ U . . .

RESPECT POWER

Hey Baby, hey baby. Slow it Down.
Let me show you the Steps of Love. Awww . . .
How Precious; your taking baby steps . . .
Now come a little closer . . . Step one may be tricky . . . ooops . . .
Don't Fall . . . Two baby two . . . Now, take that off.
Don't be Shy, Step 3's a stride.
Confidence is yours, as My Chest Pounds (bump bump). Hungering
for your tongue inside.
Slewrp ummm . . . Taste it so Good. My needs to travail you as Hard
as Wood. Knock-Knock* . . . Step four a cumbersome task. Open
up let me in "Shouldnist I" . . . as the door slams . . . Quickly in . . .
Maybe to take your breath away, or was it just the Wind. The screen
door squeaks . . . Fallacies ignite! . . . As Aroma fills the air . . .
Sweet Philosophies find you dare!
Are you Dreaming now? . . .
Just to wake you dreaming! . . .
Keep going you're doing just Fine. You are almost there . . .
>---}-->Loverboy@U

DELIBERATE

You Don't Know non' bout Real Love . . .
Real Love is Slow . . .
Do You know how Much Real Love Cost?
Walking Down this Country Road.
So, Go Steak your Claim
This Land is My land
You Don't know non' bout Real Love
Growl with Fever . . . Now Forever More . . .
Now Forever Moe

NUDE

You been My homegirl for so Long
You know you been My Queen . . . Ace in the Hole; Ace of
Spades . . . Unless you count the Duece, and Da Diva . . .
Never need a Joker or a King!
>---}-->Loverboy@U

?

We could call it something else . . .
What you want to call it?
Love . . . ? . . . ha ha
Really? Don't be Silly (eyebrow raised)
About Us.
The More you know the Better you Live . . .
>---}-->Loverboy@U

Some Beings Are Perfect . . . "You just have to Know It."

Give thanks to my Ghost Writer, "Loverboy >--}-->@" . . . He is evolving into a spirit of his own liking. The bow and arrow symbol is the symbol of the Sagittarius. He carries it wherever he goes. It's the same bow and arrow that Cupid carries. So, "BEWARE" not to get struck by the arrow of Love. For the arrow of Love sees no Race, Gender, or Age barriers. Our President, Barrack Obama is a prime example of the powers of Love. Being the product of a Bi-racial relationship, he has taken us into the 21st Century with an openness and candor that only Destiny could purpose. With all the racial tensions of the past and present, we all have to realize that we wake up under the same Sun every morning and we sleep under the same Moon each night until the day we die. O'er *Erogenous Moon*

EROGENOUS MOON

EROGENOUS MOON, FIRMAMENT INDUCED INTRICATE PLEASURES. SPONTANEOUS IMPULSES BEYOND ALL MEASURE; AROUSED BY NATURE. H€AR THE THUNDER ROAR!! FALL SECRET DESIRES, WE DO ADORE;' COME TO ME' SURRENDER YOUR WILL! FILL MY POWER! AS TIME STANDS STILL! FEEL THE PASSION, FEAR THE PAIN. HEAR MY HEARTBEAT, SOUNDS THE SAME. FALL FROM THE SKY, O' FULL MOON, AND LAY DOWN BESIDE ME. BRIDE AND GROOM.

This is one of my favorite poems. The moon represents the subliminal mind. The message is truly one of "Racial Harmony" in the World, and Upon the Earth. Ambiguous Desires is more than surface poetry. Its' meanings are meant to inspire the brain to react to education. The brain is an Amazing organ. Collectively it is our body's sole purpose to protect this organ. Its uncanny ability to retain information is Divine. The brains ability to repair itself is fascinating. A broken heart is really an emotionally scared brain. It just feels like it's the Heart. Picture a "Brain" with an arrow through it. It can not be repaired. But a Heart with an arrow through it, Can; through the power of the brain. They call it "Neuroplasticity." **Neuroplasticity**: The brain's ability to reorganize itself by forming new neural connections throughout life.

I am a single father. "With only one begotten son," Whosoever believes in him shall have everlasting Life. My son was born on January 4, 2000. He was the sixth child born in Hamilton, Ohio (Butler County). He was a "New Millennium Baby." I named him JahMaudi Isaiah; however, his mom named him the name my mom named me "Coary". What a compromise, that's what life is all about. I settled for that, and tell him the story of his birth, and his real name every chance I get. He is my world! Luckily, his middle name is "JahMaudi" which means "Son of God." A good name is better than precious ointment; and the day of death than the day of one's birth (Ecclesiastes 7:1) King James Version. A good name is more desirable than great riches; to be esteemed is better than silver or gold (Proverbs 22:1) New International Version. I know; the heartbreak, pain, and loneliness of not being able to share a father and son's bond. The snake in the Garden of Eden is a representation of this misfortune on Mankind. No one ever discusses what a father, who loves his child, may feel inside! "Loosing a child" not literally, but figuratively speaking! **Figurative** Representing by a figure, or by resemblance; typical; representative.

This, they will say, was figurative, and served, by God's appointment, but for a time, to shadow out the True glory of a more divine sanctity.

"Loosing a child to the structure of society," "Loosing a child to the Workforce." (Neglect). Recently, the 2013 Boston Marathon was bombed by some children, who were brainwashed to believe that hurting others would cure their pains. Reportedly, approximately 3 people were killed, and over 282 people were injured in two separate blasts. The day my son was born was the happiest day of my life! When my son was 14 days old, I was taken away from my only beloved. I fell into a deep depression which drained me of all "My True feelings!" Depression is a serious illness of the mind. Until the brain restores itself, it can lead a person to series of pitfalls. I use the analogy of the "Spinning Coin." It takes a repetition of circular motions before reaching "Rock Bottom." Once it makes a complete stop, you can no longer hear the sound. A ring rin rin rinr irn rin ririrn rinrinr rinr! Faster and faster . . . You do not know your there (bottom) until after the Fact. A depressed person will not say "I'm depressed" because as my mom, Judgella Parham Goode would say, "you don't know; what you don't know!" We can be swept away with the tolls of Life, Illiteracy, Unemployment, Poverty, Addiction, and Homelessness. During the recession of 2008, many middle class people lost their homes, and found themselves without jobs. "Sometimes the Bell Tolls for Thee;" Never the less, I opened my eyes, and realized that it was time for me to live again.

I am a licensed cosmetologist. I have been active in my Profession for 22 years. I opened up my business, "Salon7Spa," during the recession of 2008-2012. My rent and utilities would run me $1000's each month, but I had a passion for my Profession. When my business was struggling, I found leisure in writing poetry. I had to sleep in my salon to keep it going. The 7 in salon7spa stands for the 7 colors of the Rainbow, (Red, Orange, Yellow, Green, Blue, Indigo, and Violet). It also stands for the fact that I was open 24-7, 24 hours a day and 7 days a week. I managed to go to Church on Saturday or Sunday when ever it was convenient. Yes, I met scrutiny from the 7 day Adventist church that I attended, but I left them with the parable . . . Then He answered them, saying, "Which of you, having a donkey or an ox that has fallen into a pit, will not immediately pull him out on the Sabbath day" (Luke 14:5) King James Version? They say 7 is the number of completion. I realized that I was depressed seven years after the birth of my son. My rent and utilities would run me $1000's each month, but I had a passion for my Profession. I was the owner/operator. "I Woke Up!" Spike Lee coined the phrase "WAKE UP" in a classic Movie called School Daze. My fellow Americans, Sistas and Brothas it's time to "WAKE UP," and get an "Education." My poetry inspired me to continue my education. Not only would I write poetry when business was slow, I would also attend online classes in between clients. At the age of 42, I will be graduating in March, 2014 with an Associate's Degree in General Studies. Writing poetry inspired me to continue my education. Ambiguous Desires is the awakening of my suppressed emotions!

Thank you, for purchasing my book, not only are you buying a book, you are breaking generational curses, and supporting a "Dream!"

Coary L.